This edition published in 2022 by Palazzo Editions Ltd
15 Church Road
London, SW13 9HE
www.palazzoeditions.com

First published in 2019 by Carlton Books Ltd

Design, text and layout © 2019 Palazzo Editions Limited

All rights reserved. No part of this publication may be reproduced in any form or by any means — electronic, mechanical, photocopying, recording, or otherwise — or stored in any retrieval system of any nature without prior written permission from the copyright holders. Colin Stuart has asserted his moral right to be identified as the author of this work in accordance with the Copyright Designs and Patents Act of 1988.

A CIP catalogue record for this book is available from the British Library.

ISBN 9781786750747

Manufactured in the UK

10 9 8 7 6 5 4 3 2 1

Designs, illustrations and editing by Dynamo Ltd

For Harrison,

GO ON A MISSION TO
MARS

Colin Stuart

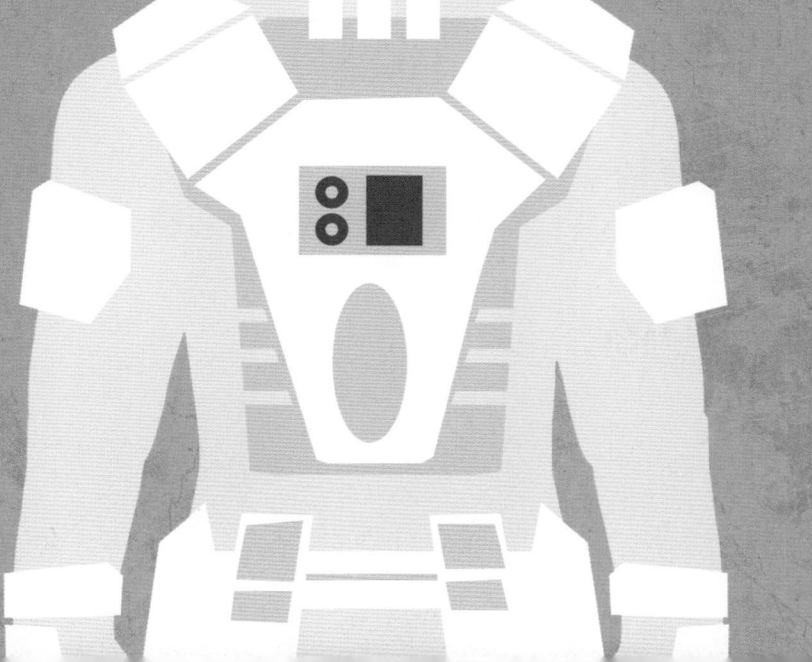

MISSION TO MARS

Nobody has ever made a journey to Mars. So far only robots have visited this fascinating red planet, but plans are now being made for the first human adventure.

This guide will give you the information you need to take part in a trip yourself. Once you arrive you might be able to solve the greatest Martian mystery of all — is there life already on Mars?

Are you brave enough?
Are you smart enough?

OF COURSE YOU ARE!
LET'S GO!

INSIDE YOUR GUIDE

LEARN ABOUT MARS

8 The adventure starts here
10 Mars — the story
12 Martian seasons
14 Robot visitors
16 Mars moons
18 Danger!

MAKE THE JOURNEY

20 Your training
22 Your onboard guide
24 Arriving

EXPLORING MARS

26 Eating and breathing
28 Look down, look up
30 Search for liquid water
32 Landscape highlights
34 Craters, plateaus and dunes
36 Ice and gas clues
38 Terraforming Mars

MISSION ACCOMPLISHED

40 Coming home
42 Mars dreaming
44 Glossary

THE ADVENTURE STARTS HERE

An incredible journey to Mars awaits. This book will give you all the background you need to plan your space adventure.

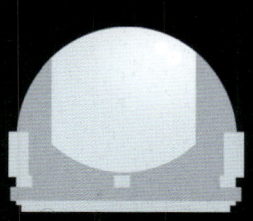  Find out about your astronaut training.

Read about how to survive on Mars, including growing your own food, and collecting water.

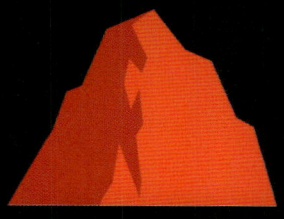 Discover some of the breathtaking sights on Mars, such as towering mountains and deep canyons.

Read all about the plans for the future on Mars.

GOOD LUCK ON YOUR SPACEFLIGHT!

MARS VITAL STATS

DIAMETER:
6,779 KM

= 53% of Earth's

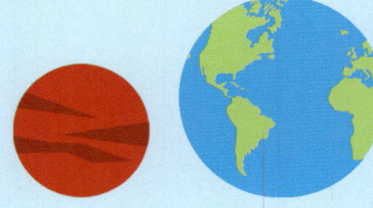

MASS:
640,000 MILLION TRILLION KILOGRAMS

= 10.7% of Earth's

 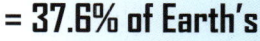

SURFACE GRAVITY:

= 37.6% of Earth's

ATMOSPHERIC PRESSURE:
0.00628 ATM
(EARTH = 1 ATM)

= 0.6% of Earth's

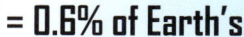 

MOONS: x 2

 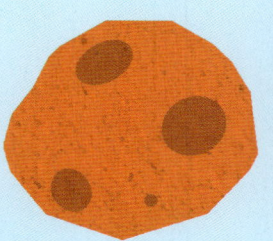

Deimos   Phobos

LEARN ABOUT MARS

Mars is the fourth planet from the sun in the solar system.

PLUTO (DWARF PLANET)
NEPTUNE
URANUS
JUPITER
SATURN
MARS
EARTH
VENUS
MERCURY
SUN

MARS'S ATMOSPHERE

The gases in the atmosphere on Mars would make it deadly to breathe.

95.97%	CARBON DIOXIDE
1.93%	ARGON
1.89%	NITROGEN
0.15%	OXYGEN
0.06%	CARBON MONOXIDE

MARS IS A MINIMUM OF

54 MILLION KM

FROM EARTH

DEADLY! BREATHING APPARATUS NEEDED

MARS – THE STORY

Mars has had a fascinating history stretching back billions of years, and there is one big mystery still to solve.

MARS IS BORN

① Around five billion years ago a gigantic cloud of gas and dust collapsed under its own weight. Temperatures and pressure soared and a new star was born — the sun. Leftover material began spinning round the new star.

② The material started clumping together to form large chunks. They collided with each other to form planets. In the inner solar system rocky planets such as Mars formed.

③ The heaviest materials, such as metals, sank to the middle of the new planet Mars. The outer layer cooled to form a crust. The pressure of the top layers kept the inside of the planet molten hot, and there were lots of volcanoes.

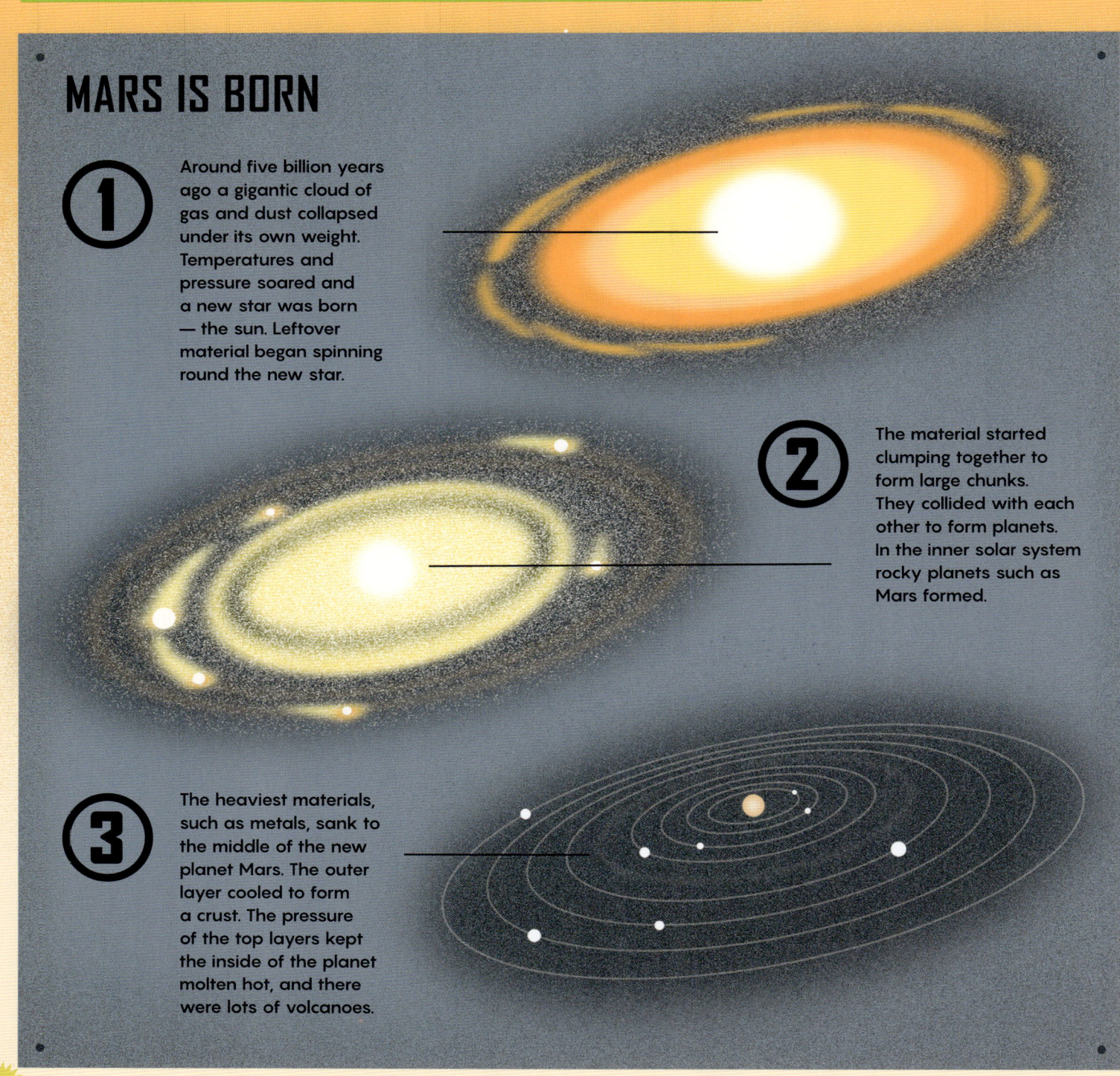

LEARN ABOUT MARS

FROM OCEANS TO DESERT

It's thought that long ago Mars had deep oceans, but now it is mostly a dusty desert. So what happened? It's likely to be the fault of the solar wind — a gale of charged particles that blows from the sun. Mars has a much weaker magnetic field than Earth because its inner core cooled down (Earth has a super-hot core). Without this protection, the solar wind may have gradually destroyed the atmosphere on Mars, so most of its water disappeared. The remaining water is largely frozen at the poles of the planet.

Mars may once have had deep oceans, so did it have life and, if so, does it still exist?

THE BIG QUESTION ?
IS / WAS THERE LIFE ON MARS?

MARTIAN SEASONS

On your Martian adventure you won't find the same seasons that you would experience on Earth. Here are the differences to expect.

PERIHELION

The nearest point to the sun of the Mars orbit is called *perihelion*. At perihelion it is winter in the north and summer in the south. Southern summers are hot and short, and the temperature can trigger gigantic dust storms that can envelop the whole planet for weeks.

Mars takes nearly twice as long to orbit the sun than Earth. Its year lasts **687 days**.

Mars orbits the sun in a stretched-out oval shape, much more stretched than Earth's orbit. This gives it unusual seasons.

A year on Earth lasts **365 days**.

EARTH

THE SUN

On Earth, the seasonal weather is broadly similar in both the north and south. Summers are roughly as warm, and winters are similarly cold in both the northern and southern hemispheres.

You'll have to get used to considerably lower light levels on Mars. The sunlight is on average only around 40 per cent as intense as it is on Earth.

LEARN ABOUT MARS

APHELION

The furthest point of the orbit is called *aphelion*. At aphelion it is summer in the northern hemisphere, but there's a long cold winter in the south. Don't expect Earth-summer temperatures in the north, though. It's bone-chillingly cold most of the time.

MARTIAN SEASON LENGTHS
(northern hemisphere)

SPRING	SUMMER
7 months	**6** months
AUTUMN	WINTER
5 months	**4** months

Temperatures can reach a balmy 35°C at the equator during Martian summer, but they can also plummet to an inhospitable -143°C at the poles in winter. Average temperatures are a frosty -63°C.

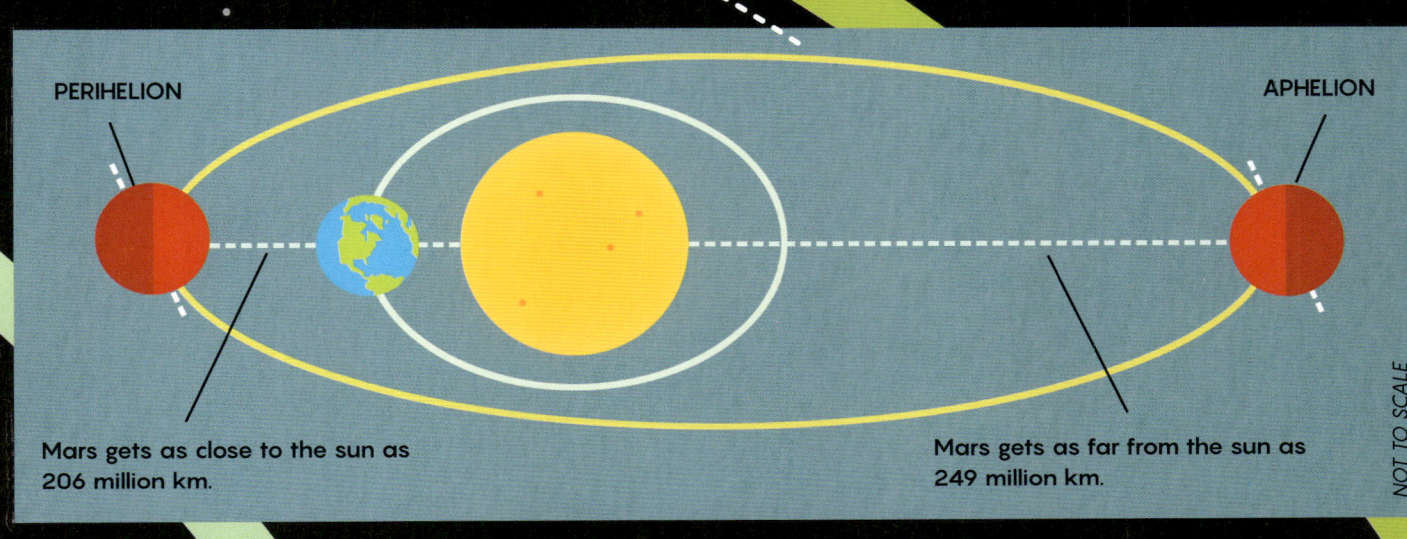

PERIHELION — Mars gets as close to the sun as 206 million km.

APHELION — Mars gets as far from the sun as 249 million km.

NOT TO SCALE

TRAVEL ADVICE: AVOID FREEZING ON MARS. ONLY EVER VENTURE OUTSIDE WITH THE CORRECT PROTECTIVE EQUIPMENT, WHATEVER THE SEASON.

ROBOT VISITORS

Robot probes have visited Mars and helped to map out areas of the planet.

MARINER 4

1964-1971

NASA's *Mariner 4* probe was launched in 1964. It flew past Mars and returned the first close-up photos. *Mariner 9* reached Mars in 1971 and revealed more of the surface.

1975

NASA launched the *Viking 1* and *Viking 2* missions. Both touched down in 1976. They sent back stunning images of the vivid red surface and used their robotic arms to take samples for onboard experiments.

1997

The NASA *Sojourner* rover landed on Mars. Unlike the static *Vikings* it could use its six wheels to move around from site to site. It drilled into rocks and took almost 10 million measurements of the wind and atmosphere on Mars.

OLYMPUS MONS — Giant volcano

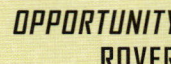

SOLOS PLANUM

VALLES MARINERIS — Canyon system

ARGYRA PLANITIA

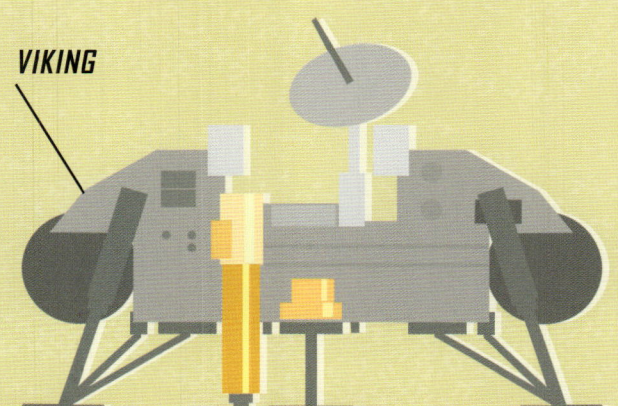

VIKING

SOJOURNER ROVER

OPPORTUNITY ROVER

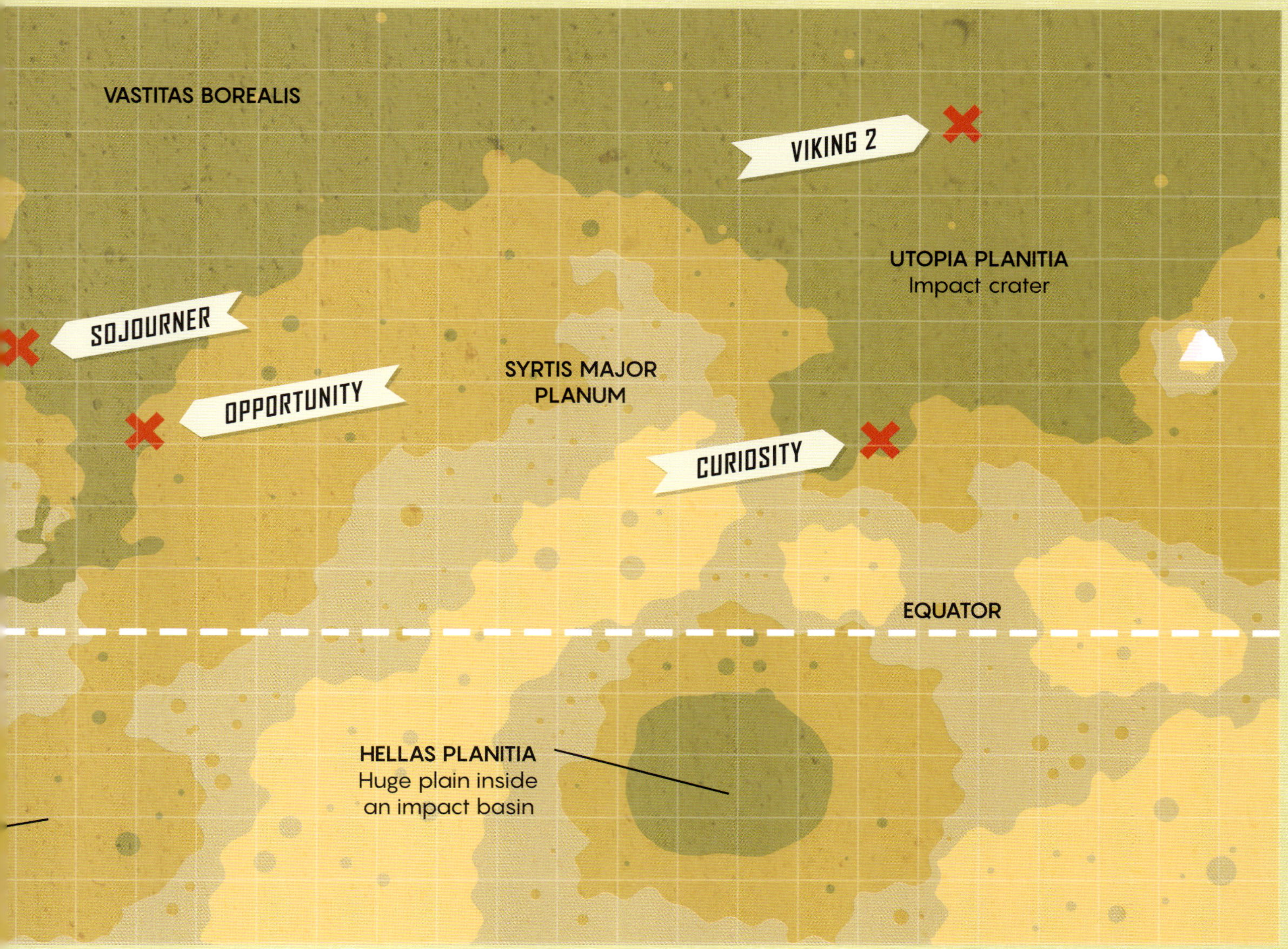

LEARN ABOUT MARS

VASTITAS BOREALIS

VIKING 2

UTOPIA PLANITIA
Impact crater

SOJOURNER

OPPORTUNITY

SYRTIS MAJOR PLANUM

CURIOSITY

EQUATOR

HELLAS PLANITIA
Huge plain inside an impact basin

2004

The NASA *Spirit* and *Opportunity* rovers touched down, mapped areas of the planet and found evidence of past water.

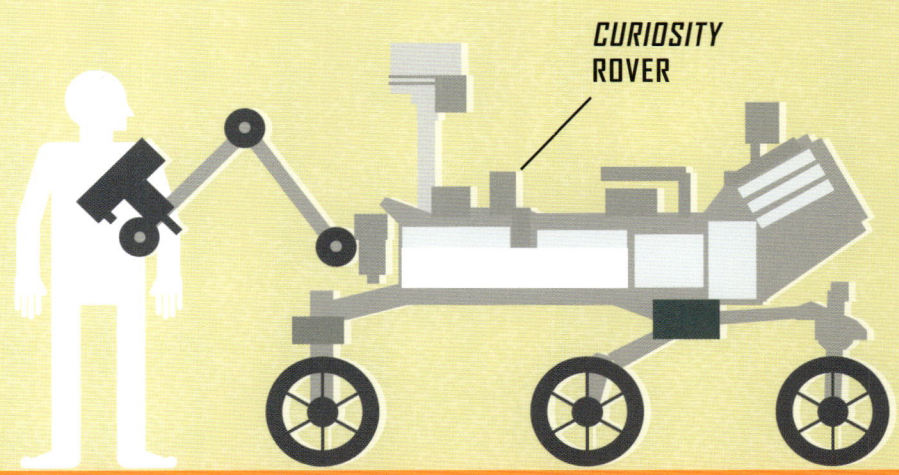

CURIOSITY ROVER

2012

The car-sized *Curiosity* rover landed on Mars. Previous probes were dropped to the surface inside air bags, but the much larger *Curiosity* was gently lowered onto the surface using a sky crane — a rocket-powered descent vehicle.

15

MARS MOONS

Mars has two tiny moons, some of the smallest in the solar system.

PHOBOS

DEIMOS

MOON DISCOVERY

American astronomer Asaph Hall nearly gave up his search for the moons of Mars but his wife Angeline persuaded him to carry on. He eventually spotted Phobos and Deimos through his telescope in Washington DC in 1877.

Mars is named after the Roman god of war. The moons are named after his sons.

The moons' names mean 'terror' (Deimos) and 'fear' (Phobos). They are named after the twin sons of Mars, the Roman god of war. The Romans named the planet after the war god because of its blood-red colour.

LEARN ABOUT MARS

PHOBOS FACTS

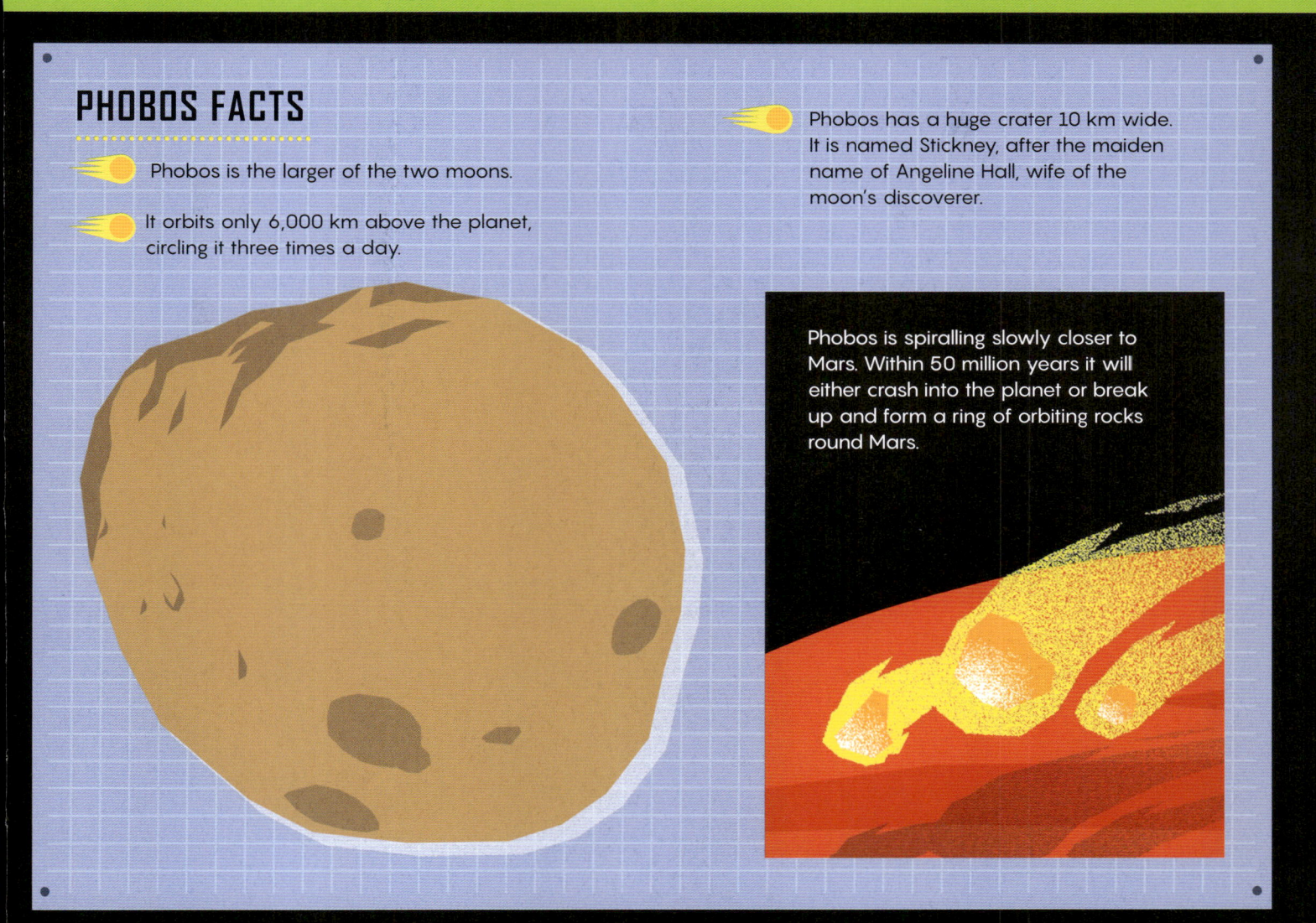

- Phobos is the larger of the two moons.
- It orbits only 6,000 km above the planet, circling it three times a day.
- Phobos has a huge crater 10 km wide. It is named Stickney, after the maiden name of Angeline Hall, wife of the moon's discoverer.

Phobos is spiralling slowly closer to Mars. Within 50 million years it will either crash into the planet or break up and form a ring of orbiting rocks round Mars.

DEIMOS FACTS

- Deimos is further away from Mars than Phobos. It takes 30 hours to go round the planet.
- It is 12 km wide.
- Like Phobos, it is lumpy, heavily cratered and littered with rocks and dust.
- Scientists have discussed using one of the moons as a base for sending robot vehicles to Mars, since the base would be partly shielded from dangerous cosmic and solar radiation.

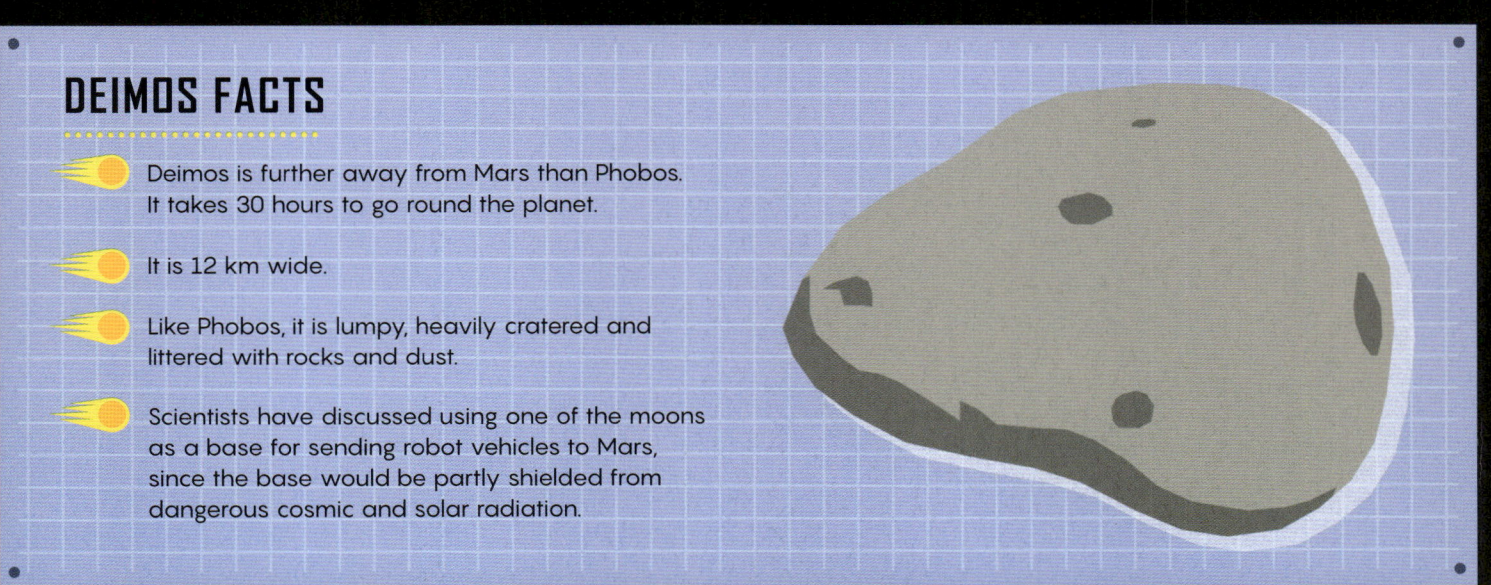

DANGER!

Mars will be a highly dangerous place to visit. Here are some of the problems visitors will have to cope with.

RADIATION

The sun and other stars in the galaxy send out a deadly stream of particles that can damage body tissue. Our bodies are shielded from it by the atmosphere and magnetic field that wrap around the Earth, but Mars has no such shield. Prolonged stays won't be advisable and any buildings will need to have thick radiation shields.

MENTAL HARDSHIP

Visitors will have to deal with the knowledge that their loved ones are far away in space, and around seven months' journey away. Messages take at least 12.5 minutes to reach Earth, so conversation isn't easy. Travellers will also have to get used to living in a small space with their colleagues and learn to cope with any arguments that happen.

It would be a good idea to set up a spare emergency habitat to escape to if necessary, with stocks of food and air.

LEARN ABOUT MARS

METEORS

Meteors tend to burn up when they reach Earth's atmosphere, but on Mars many make it through. Mars is hit around 200 times more often than Earth. Any buildings will need to be meteorite-proof, and some kind of large meteorite warning system might have to be set up on the planet surface.

200 number of objects bigger than **one metre** that hit the planet yearly.

1 MEGATON Occasionally an object hits the planet with a force equal to **one megaton of TNT**.

DUST STORMS

Dust storms as big as continents rage for weeks across the planet, covering everything in red particles and blocking out the sun. Unlike on Earth, there is no rain to clear the air after a storm, so it remains filled with choking dust for a long time.

In 2018 NASA reported that a dust storm had grown to completely cover the entire planet.

YOUR TRAINING

A trip to Mars is no ordinary holiday. You'll need astronaut training and medical checks before you can book your place on the launch vehicle.

ENGINEERING

You will be given engineering training, to learn how to operate and mend your equipment.

TRAINING SCHEDULE

You will be trained and tested in a neutral buoyancy tank, a large pool of water that is designed to simulate micro-gravity.

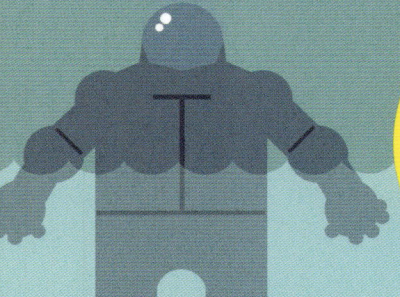

Can you tread water for 10 continuous minutes wearing a flight suit?

Can you swim 75m (246 ft.) without stopping, wearing an astronaut flight suit and tennis shoes?

MEDICAL

You will learn first aid and the best way to use onboard medicines.

TEAMWORK

You will be given training to help you get along with your team and work effectively together.

THE *VOMIT COMET*

You will be taken up in the vomit comet — an aeroplane that flies in loops to simulate weightlessness in space. You may find yourself being sick, hence the nickname of the plane.

20

MAKE THE JOURNEY

CENTRIFUGE

You will be spun round in a giant centrifuge to simulate the high acceleration you will experience during the launch.

HAPPINESS

During your Mars journey you will be away from home for months. You will be given training to cope with home sickness and unhappy feelings.

MARS TERRAIN

You will train on a realistic mock-up of the surface of Mars. This may be in an isolated desert location.

MOUNTAINS

DUST

Once you have passed your training you can go on the next available flight.

YOUR MEDICAL CHECK

You'll need to be healthy and fit to go on the trip because you won't be able to get to hospital up in space. Here's what your medical form will need to look like.

- Free of disease ✓
- Good eyesight ✓
- Not too tall or too heavy ✓
- Good blood pressure. 140/90 sitting down. ✓

Current astronaut heights are set between 1.48m and 1.9m.

Spacecraft are small, and extra weight means extra fuel costs, so astronauts are usually under 81.6 kg in weight.

21

YOUR ONBOARD GUIDE

On your trip to Mars you will be on your spaceship for several months. The rocket shown is the type of craft that might be built to take you.

MARS EXPLORER

MARS EXPLORER　　**SPACE SHUTTLE**

Passengers will need to share cabins as space will be tight. There will be communal areas for entertainment, a communal galley (kitchen) and a gym.

The payload area is where travellers will live and supplies will be stored.

There will be a solar storm shelter on board where passengers will be protected from any radiation from solar flares — sudden eruptions of energy from the surface of the sun.

Carbon fibre fuel tanks will need to be refuelled on the surface of Mars.

Delta (triangular) wings could help control the pitch and roll of the ship as it nears Mars.

Engines will accelerate the ship to speeds of 100,000 km/h.

MAKE THE JOURNEY

ONBOARD LIFE

You will need to exercise for two to four hours a day to counteract the loss of muscle and bone strength that comes from living in a weightless environment. Without this, your body will begin to waste away.

Meals will be pre-packed and designed to last for several months. The menu will be mainly reconstituted dried food or protein bars, though it may be possible to grow some salad lettuce under lights.

Scientists are working on new skin-tight pressurized spacesuit designs.

When you near Mars you will be asked to put on your pressurized spacesuit ready for landing. The low pressure on the surface of Mars would instantly cause your blood to boil, so these suits must be worn whenever you go outside, along with your helmet and breathing system.

ARRIVING

Here's what to expect when you finally land on the surface of the planet.

LANDING

Touchdown on Mars isn't easy. As it hurtles down through the thin atmosphere, the outer shell of a landing craft could reach temperatures of up to 1,700 °C.

① The landing craft will come down rapidly.

The craft will be designed to withstand that heat, but the big problem will be successfully braking.

② Supersonic boosters will fire as it nears the surface.

Small craft such as robot probes can be slowed by parachutes and airbags, but a big landing craft will need supersonic retro-propulsion boosters to fire and slow it down.

③ Landing feet must deploy to prevent the craft from toppling over.

24

MAKE THE JOURNEY

LAVA CAVE

YOUR CAMP

Any Martian settlement will have to cope with tough conditions and deadly daily threats to survival.

It might be a good idea to set up camp underground, perhaps in the caves at the base of the Pavonis Mons volcano. These are tubes created long ago by flows of lava that carved out hollow tunnels. Photos of these have shown up a few holes that would act as skylights, letting light through from above.

Before you go to Mars, you can experience lava tubes on Earth. Astronauts have trained in lava tubes on the Canary Islands.

DANGERS ON MARS'S SURFACE

 **METEORITES**

 **COSMIC RADIATION**
 FROM STARS

 **DUST STORMS**

25

EATING AND BREATHING

The Martian atmosphere doesn't contain the oxygen that humans need to breathe. Nor is it possible for plants to grow there or farm animals to survive. So how will you breathe and what will you eat on your trip?

Easy-to-grow high-yielding crops will be planted.

POTATOES

PEAS

SWEETCORN

RADISHES

DOWN ON THE FARM (MARTIAN-STYLE)

Food will probably be grown in specially constructed greenhouse domes. Inside the plants might be grown *hydroponically* — in a solution of water and nutrients instead of soil.

It would take too much work and resources to keep herds of farm animals for food, but it might be possible to farm edible insects to give Mars inhabitants a protein source. Crickets have almost as much protein as beef.

It's possible that Martian soil could be used to grow crops if poisonous chemicals were removed from it and nutrients were added.

EXPLORING MARS

OXYGEN ON MARS

Humans breathe in eight litres of air a minute and almost 21 per cent of that is oxygen.

We will need to set up oxygen-making factories to cope with the demand, perhaps using the idea shown below.

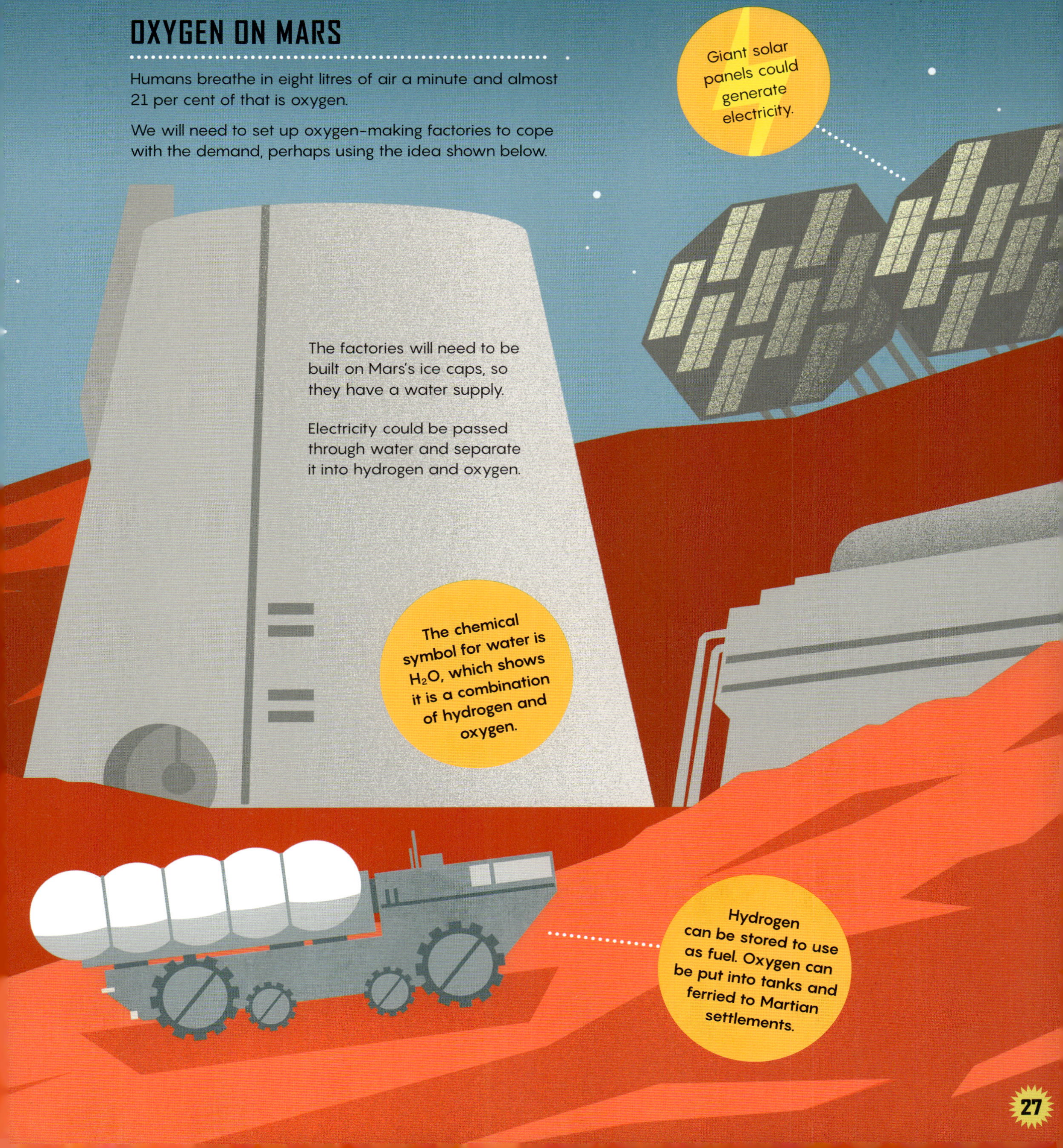

Giant solar panels could generate electricity.

The factories will need to be built on Mars's ice caps, so they have a water supply.

Electricity could be passed through water and separate it into hydrogen and oxygen.

The chemical symbol for water is H_2O, which shows it is a combination of hydrogen and oxygen.

Hydrogen can be stored to use as fuel. Oxygen can be put into tanks and ferried to Martian settlements.

27

LOOK DOWN, LOOK UP

What will you see beneath your feet and above your head on Mars?

THE RUSTY PLANET

Mars is famous for its red appearance, caused by a layer of iron-oxide dust. On Earth we call it rust! Mars has very iron-rich rocks, which fierce winds have worn down to create the dust. Beneath this red layer the rocks are hard basalt, formed by the rapid cooling of volcanic lava when Mars was a young planet.

DUSTY DUNES

At certain times during the Martian year the temperature warms up, causing violent winds of up to 400 km/h. These sculpt loose sand into big sand dunes. Sometimes there are giant sand avalanches.

DUST COMING!

The wind might whip the dust into moving whirling funnels called dust devils. These occur in deserts on Earth.

EXPLORING MARS

THE MARTIAN SKY

Star-gazing will be a treat on Mars because there won't be any light pollution, as there often is on Earth. You will be able to see Earth as a tiny blue dot, with its moon nearby. The moon Phobos will be easy to see as it orbits Mars, occasionally passing across the sun (see page 16).

PHOBOS

EARTH

VENUS

SPIDER-WEB CHANNELS

When spring comes to the southern polar ice cap, gas comes out from under the ice, creating holes like Swiss cheese and strange spider-like patterns called *araneiforms*, which are seen nowhere else in the solar system.

An araneiform, channels radiating out from a pit.

SEARCH FOR LIQUID WATER

Most of the water on Mars is in the form of ice at the poles, but does it have flowing water? Here is the evidence so far. Perhaps human visitors will one day find out once and for all.

CANALS? NO

Astronomers once saw criss-crossing straight lines on Mars and believed they were canals built by mysterious Martians. They turned out to be just an optical illusion.

CHLORIDE? YES

Probes have spotted deposits of chloride on Mars, a chemical that is left behind when water evaporates away. It's evidence that water disappeared from Mars in the past.

People once thought there were canals built by aliens on Mars.

SALTY STREAKS

Most of the water on Mars is at the poles in the form of ice, but in 2015 something unusual was spotted inside the Garni Crater, a large impact site on the planet's surface. Temporary long dark streaks were spotted running down the inside of the crater. It's possible these might be caused by liquid water, which would have to be salty to avoid freezing (salty water freezes at a lower temperature than fresh water).

GARNI CRATER

EXPLORING MARS

WHAT'S BENEATH?

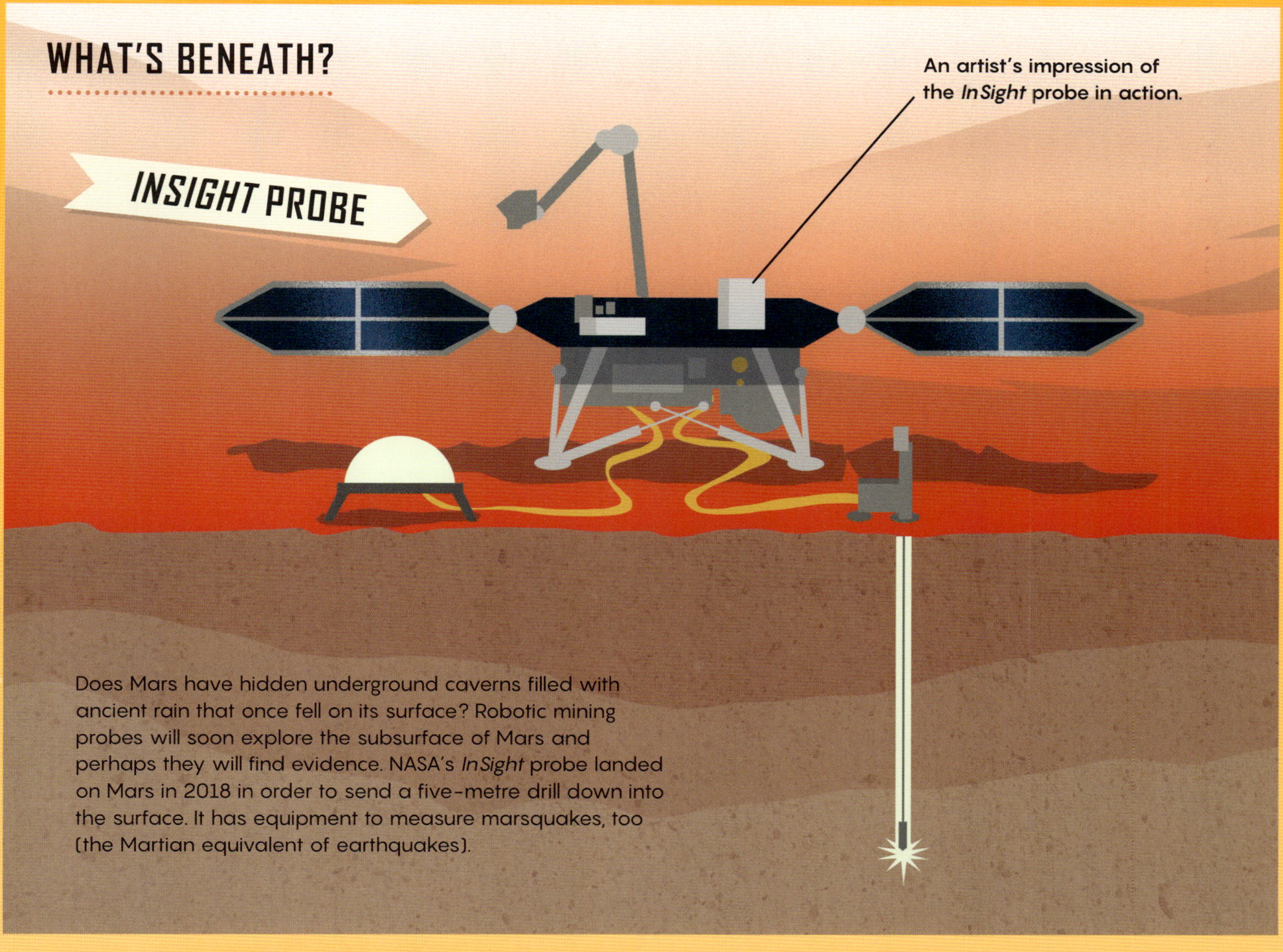

INSIGHT PROBE

An artist's impression of the *InSight* probe in action.

Does Mars have hidden underground caverns filled with ancient rain that once fell on its surface? Robotic mining probes will soon explore the subsurface of Mars and perhaps they will find evidence. NASA's *InSight* probe landed on Mars in 2018 in order to send a five-metre drill down into the surface. It has equipment to measure marsquakes, too (the Martian equivalent of earthquakes).

DUSTY ICE

Mars has slow-moving ice glaciers, but they're hidden beneath a thick layer of dust. In 2018, NASA released images of hidden ice cliffs, too.

HIDDEN GLACIER

LANDSCAPE HIGHLIGHTS

The spectacular landscape on Mars includes huge towering volcanoes and incredibly deep canyons.

OLYMPUS MONS

This giant extinct volcano is near a huge plateau called the Tharsis bulge that covers 25 per cent of the planet. There are other volcanoes here, too, all higher than any mountain on Earth.

The slopes of Olympus Mons are shallow, so it would be possible to climb it, though this would take weeks on foot. At the summit there is a huge volcanic crater called a *caldera*.

The volcano's crater is over **60 km** wide and **3 km** deep.

21,287 m above datum (zero elevation)

OLYMPUS MONS

8,844 m above sea level

MOUNT EVEREST

EXPLORING MARS

Welcome to the HELLAS IMPACT CRATER

This massive crater is so huge that Mount Everest would only just peek out over its rim.

It was probably created by a huge object smashing into the planet around 3.9 billion years ago.

The crater has its own hills and deep channels, probably created when Mars flowed with water.

2,300km (1,430 miles) wide

Greetings from VALLES MARINERIS

This steep-sided canyon system stretches over a vast area 4,000 km long.

The canyons were probably created when the planet's surface cracked open.

They might make a good rock-climbing location for visitors. Martian rock is mainly volcanic basalt, with plenty of good steps and handholds.

Over 200km wide and 7km deep in places.

CRATERS, PLATEAUS AND DUNES

Visitors to Mars may one day be able to rock-climb on its craters and plateaus, or dune buggy over its sand dunes.

UP TO THE PLATEAU

Syrtis Major Planum is a huge ancient plateau, so large it can be spotted by telescopes as a dark spot on the surface of Mars. People once thought it was a shallow sea or even some kind of forest.

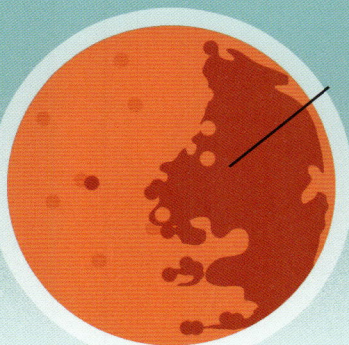

Syrtis Major Planum is 1,000 km by 1,500 km wide.

CRATER VISITING

If you wanted to go crater-spotting, you could try the Hesperia Planum, a region famous for its wrinkly ridges, created by ancient lava flows. It's home to lots of impact craters and a volcano called Tyrrhenus Mons that once spewed out ash and dust.

EXPLORING MARS

DUNE BUGGYING

The Bagnold dune field would be a good place to go dune-buggying on Mars. It's inside the Gale Crater, and its dunes have been sculpted by the Martian winds. The Martian *Curiosity* probe once explored here. However, because there is so little gravity on Mars, a dune buggy would go scarily high into the air every time it leapt a dune!

A buggy design based on one of the buggies used on the moon during an Apollo mission. It would be useful for travelling around Mars, and perhaps even exploring its dunes.

35

ICE AND GAS CLUES

Mars's icy glaciers may be able to provide a water supply for future missions. Its gas and rocks could provide clues to life.

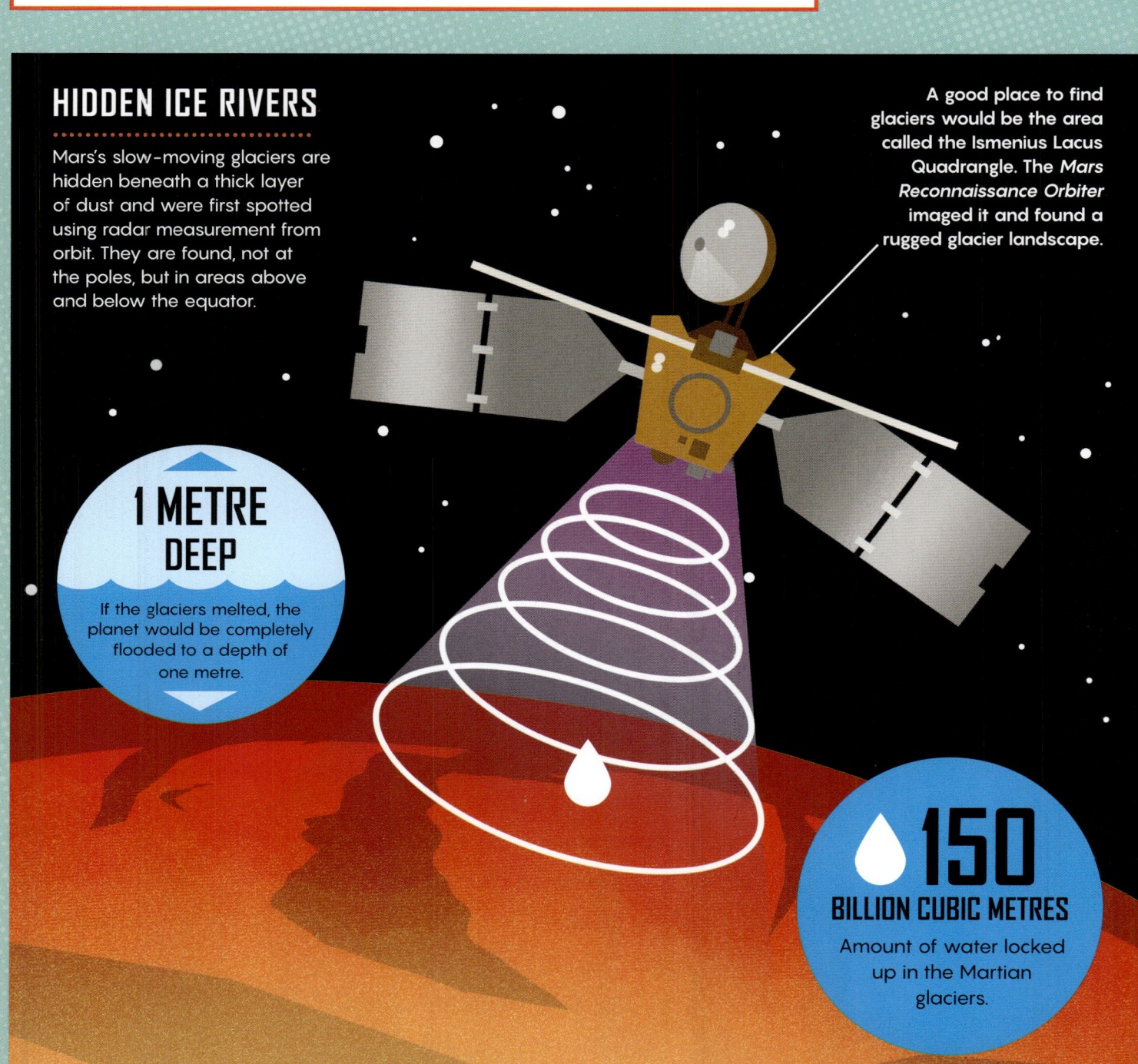

HIDDEN ICE RIVERS

Mars's slow-moving glaciers are hidden beneath a thick layer of dust and were first spotted using radar measurement from orbit. They are found, not at the poles, but in areas above and below the equator.

A good place to find glaciers would be the area called the Ismenius Lacus Quadrangle. The *Mars Reconnaissance Orbiter* imaged it and found a rugged glacier landscape.

1 METRE DEEP
If the glaciers melted, the planet would be completely flooded to a depth of one metre.

150 BILLION CUBIC METRES
Amount of water locked up in the Martian glaciers.

EXPLORING MARS

LIFE GAS

There are traces of methane gas in the Martian atmosphere. This might be a clue to life on the planet. On Earth most of our methane is produced by living things. The Martian methane could perhaps be traced back to ancient life that has since died out, or it could be from life still hidden below ground in the form of tiny microbes.

90% Proportion of Earth's methane produced by living things.

HYDROTHERMAL LIFE

It might be possible that life once existed around volcanic vents deep underwater on Mars. Earth's underwater hydrothermal vents occur where hot volcanic rocks heat up water on the seabed. They fill the water with chemicals that help keep bacteria alive.

A HYDROTHERMAL VENT ON EARTH
Ancient hydrothermal vents that were once underwater have been spotted on Mars.

LOOK, NO AIR

It's possible that bacteria exist on other planets without the need for air or light. There might even be larger creatures. The life around Earth's underwater hydrothermal vents includes giant tube worms and crabs.

HYDROTHERMAL VENTS

TERRAFORMING MARS

Scientists, novelists and film-makers dream of a Mars where humans could one day live and work comfortably. For this to happen, Mars would need to be changed to make it more Earth-like. The idea of changing a planet is called terraforming. Here are some ideas that have been suggested for doing this in the far future.

MIRRORS ON MARS

To warm up Mars and give it seas and rivers, the polar ice caps could be melted using giant orbital mirrors that direct sunlight down onto the planet.

PLANTS ON MARS

The warmed-up planet could be seeded with algae and plants. Once they begin to grow and produce oxygen, they would help transform the atmosphere.

HOTTING UP FAST

Another idea for melting the poles would be to bombard the ice with artificial meteorites carrying gases such as ammonia and methane, which would help to create a greenhouse effect — thickening and warming the atmosphere.

EXPLORING MARS

INSIDE A BUBBLE

Paraterraforming is the idea of creating a human-friendly atmosphere inside a protective shell somewhere on a planet. Inside, the atmosphere would be kept warm and creature-friendly, so plants could grow there.

An artist's impression of paraterraforming on Mars.

COMING HOME

The bad news is that nobody has figured out how to get back from a trip to Mars yet. The good news is that, given time, we humans are very good at solving problems. So would a journey to Mars be a one-way trip or would you be able to bring home souvenirs, such as a handful of rusty dust?

BLAST-OFF BY *MAV*

NASA is working on the idea of a *Mars Ascent Vehicle* — a *MAV* for short. It would take astronauts from the surface of Mars up to an *ERV* — an *Earth Return Vehicle* orbiting the planet.

A *MAV* would be too heavy to carry all the way to Mars from Earth, so it would have to be transported in pieces and constructed in space. Then it would be sent down to Mars, where it would make its own fuel by squeezing gases from the Martian atmosphere.

It would have to stand ready, able to withstand radiation and dust storms, until astronauts arrived and needed to use it.

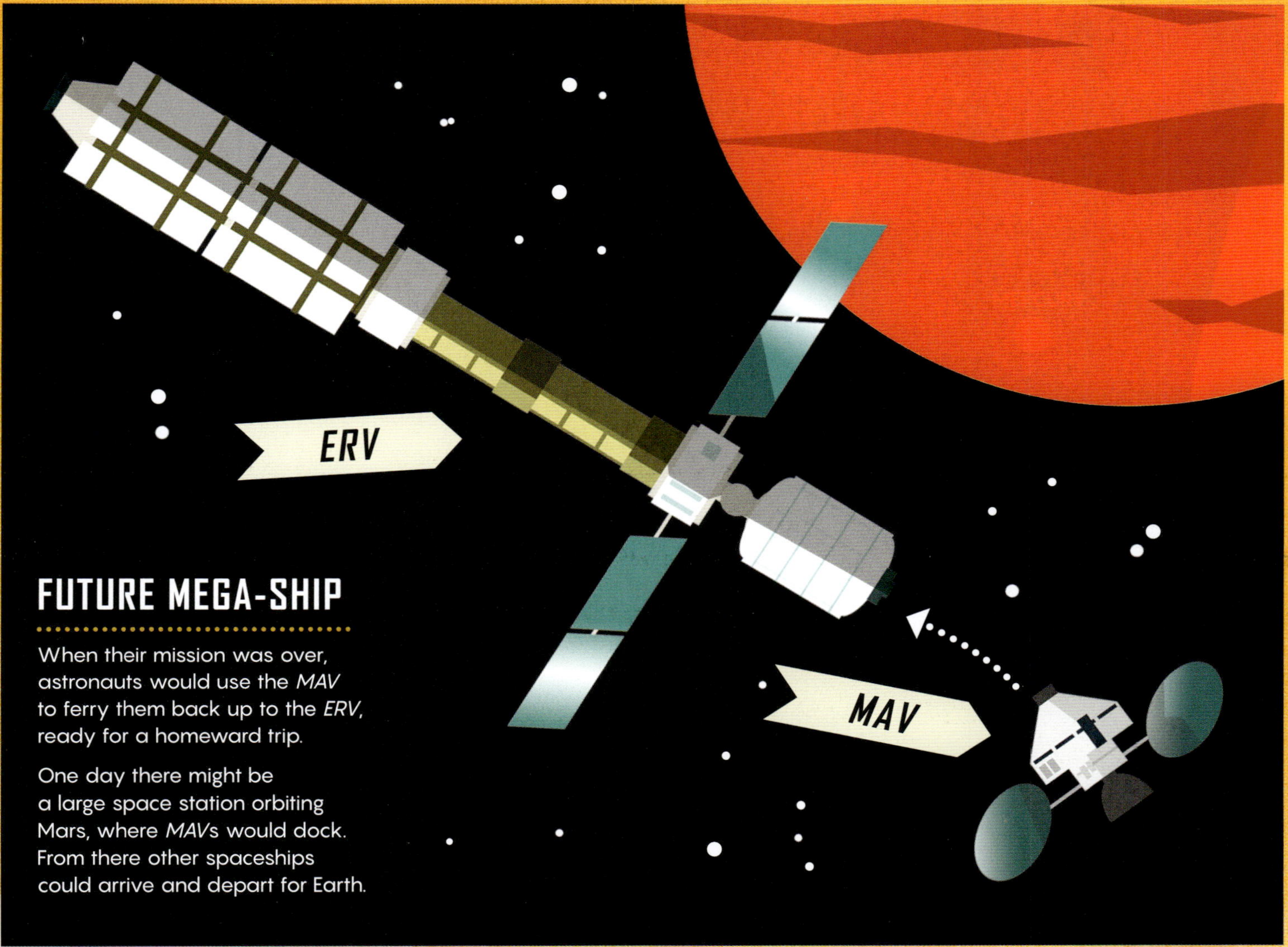

MISSION ACCOMPLISHED

ERV

MAV

FUTURE MEGA-SHIP

When their mission was over, astronauts would use the *MAV* to ferry them back up to the *ERV*, ready for a homeward trip.

One day there might be a large space station orbiting Mars, where *MAV*s would dock. From there other spaceships could arrive and depart for Earth.

?

BON VOYAGE

This is all speculation, and the technology will take many years to invent. Meanwhile, any astronauts who want to go to Mars might have to say goodbye to Earth forever. If you decide to go one day, good luck, and don't forget this book!

41

MARS DREAMING

Here are just a few of the many astronomers, scientists and inventors who have furthered our knowledge of Mars or dreamt of sending people there. Perhaps you will join them!

THE MAN WHO SAW MARS

The Italian astronomer Galileo was probably the first person to see Mars through a telescope. He saw the Red Planet through this new invention in 1610 and noted that Mars changed size, meaning it must be nearer or further from Earth at different times.

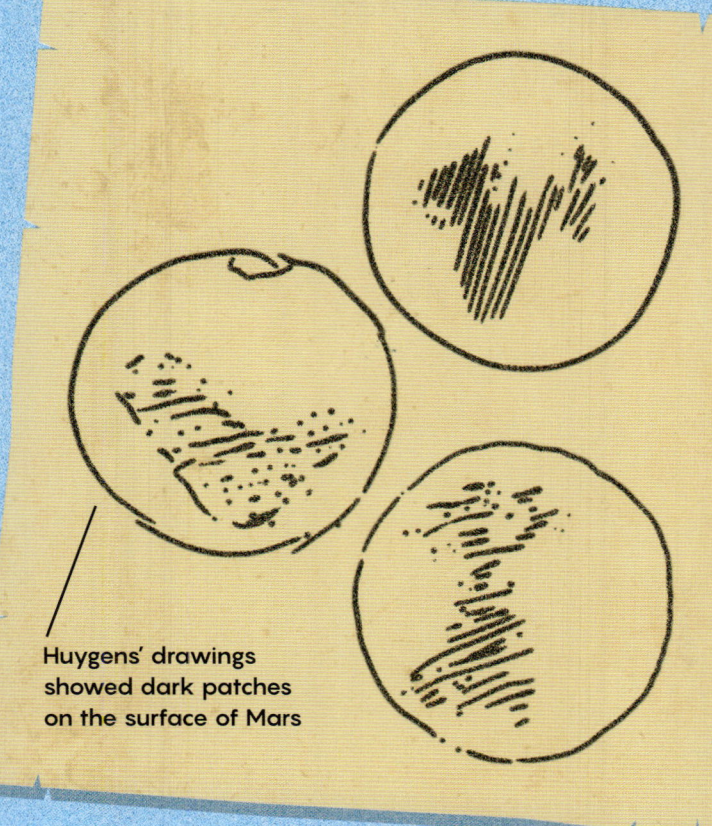

Huygens' drawings showed dark patches on the surface of Mars

GALILEO GALILEI

THE MAN WHO DREW MARS

In the 1650s, Christiaan Huygens made the first map drawings of what he saw on the surface of Mars. His sketches showed a dark region that we now know to be a big plateau called Syrtis Major Planum (see page 34). He also added one of the polar ice caps.

CARL SAGAN

THE MAN WHO SAW THE FUTURE

Carl Sagan was an American astronomer and TV star who introduced everyone to the exciting plans to study Mars. He helped with NASA's probe missions and envisaged sending rovers to Mars one day. The first one landed just a few months after his death in 1996.

MISSION ACCOMPLISHED

THE WOMAN WHO IS PLANNING A CITY

Gwynne Shotwell, president of SpaceX, plans to send people to Mars as soon as possible. She is working with entrepreneur Elon Musk and they hope to one day build on Mars and sell tickets to anyone who wants to go.

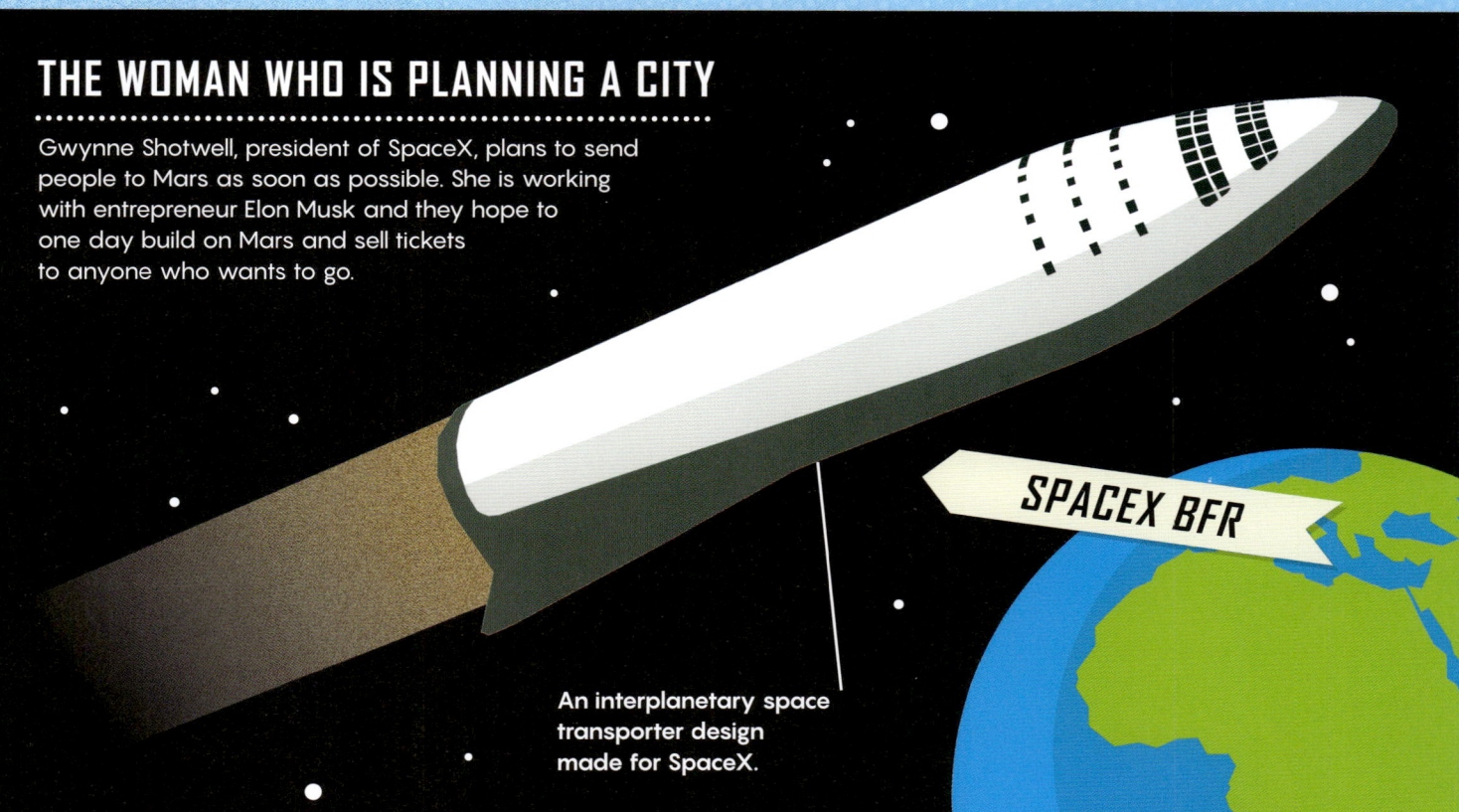

SPACEX BFR

An interplanetary space transporter design made for SpaceX.

MARS EXPERIENCE

In the meantime the United Arab Emirates has drawn up plans to build a fake Mars base in the desert near Dubai. Humans will be able to experience life on Mars there without leaving Earth.

GLOSSARY

ARANEIFORM
A pit with channels radiating out of it, found only on the surface of Mars.

ATMOSPHERE
A blanket of gases surrounding a planet.

COSMIC RADIATION
Radioactive particles coming from stars in space.

CRUST
The outer rock surface of a rocky planet.

DEIMOS
One of the two moons orbiting Mars.

EQUATOR
An imaginary line around the centre of a planet.

ERV
An *Earth Return Vehicle*, the name given to designs for spacecraft to bring people back from Mars.

GLACIERS
Slow-moving rivers of ice.

HYDROTHERMAL VENT
A location underwater where heated water bubbles around a crack in the Earth's crust. Mars once had these, too.

IMPACT CRATER
A dent in the surface of a planet made by rock hurtling in from space.

IRON OXIDE
The name given to iron particles that turn red and rusty.

LAVA
Red-hot liquid rock that spews out from underground during eruptions.

MAGNETIC FIELD
A magnetic force field that forms around planets when they are hot inside. Mars has lost its magnetic field.

GLOSSARY

MAV
A *Mars Ascent Vehicle*, the name given to designs for a Mars landing craft.

METEOR
A piece of rock that hurtles from space and enters a planet's atmosphere. If it hits the surface, it is renamed a meteorite.

OLYMPUS MONS
The giant volcano on Mars, the biggest in the solar system.

PARATERRAFORMING
The idea of creating an artificial environment similar to Earth inside a giant protective shell covering.

PHOBOS
One of the moons orbiting Mars.

SKY CRANE
A rocket-powered descent vehicle that was used to lower the *Curiosity* rover robot probe onto the surface of Mars.

SOLAR RADIATION
A stream of radioactive particles that come from the sun.

SOLAR SYSTEM
The planets that orbit the sun, together with their moons and the asteroids floating in the region.

SPACE PROBE
A robot spacecraft that lands on a planet to take images and carry out scientific experiments.

TERRAFORMING
The idea of changing the surface of another planet to make it look more like Earth.

THARSIS VOLCANIC RIDGE
A region of volcanoes on Mars.

VALLES MARINERIS
A big canyon system on Mars.